♡ **W9-BBY-271**

THE BOOK HOUSE    (770) 944-3275    -    PO
SHAPIRO, K/POEMS OF A JEW

POEMS OF A JEW

by Karl Shapiro    PERSON, PLACE AND THING

V-LETTER AND OTHER POEMS

ESSAY ON RIME

TRIAL OF A POET

POEMS 1940-1953

POEMS OF A JEW

By KARL SHAPIRO

# Poems of a Jew

 RANDOM HOUSE NEW YORK

First Printing

© Copyright, 1940, 1941, 1942, 1943, 1944, 1946, 1947, 1948, 1951, 1953, 1956, 1957, 1958, by Karl Shapiro.

All rights reserved under International and Pan-American Copyright Conventions. Published in New York by Random House, Inc., and in Toronto, Canada, by Random House of Canada, Limited.

Library of Congress Catalog Card Number: 58-5269

Of the poems in this collection, the following appeared originally in *The New Yorker*: "Israel," "The Phenomenon," "Christmas Eve: Australia," "V-Letter," "The Southerner," "The Progress of Faust," "The Convert." Others have appeared in *Poetry, The Partisan Review, Botteghe Oscure, What's New, Good Housekeeping*, and *Poetry London-New York*.

Manufactured in the United States of America

To My Parents

# Table of Contents

# Introduction

These poems are not for poets. They are for people who derive some strength of meaning from the writings of poets and who seek in the poet's mind some clue to their own thoughts. It is good to read poems for their own sake, but it is also good to read them as documents. These poems are documents of an obsession. This obsession, I believe, is universal and timeless; the Jew is at its center, but everyone else partakes of it.

The poems which I have collected for this volume do not provide answers or even ask questions; rather, they present the evidence as I see it, the states of mind which in my case led to the writing of poems, and which in others might lead to making money or becoming a comedian. There is no goal or objective here, unless expression is the goal itself. Poetry is everywhere at its goal, a wise critic once said. And one might add in paraphrase: the Jew is everywhere at his goal.

The Jewish Question, whatever that might be, is not my concern. Nor is Judaism. Nor is Jewry. Nor is Israel. The religious question is not my concern. I am one of those who views with disgust and disappointment the evangelism of the twentieth century and the backsliding of artists and intellectuals toward religion. The artist's contribution to religion must in the nature of things be heretical. These poems, in any case, are not religious poems but the poems of a Jew.

No one has been able to define *Jew,* and in essence this defiance of definition is the central meaning of Jewish consciousness. For to be a Jew is to be in a certain state of consciousness which is inescapable. As everyone knows, a Jew who becomes an atheist remains a Jew. A Jew who becomes a Catholic remains a Jew. Being a Jew is the consciousness of being a Jew, and the Jewish identity, with or

*ix.*

without religion, with or without history, is the significant fact. The Jew is unique among mankind, once he accepts this identity, and the word *Jew* retains its eternal shock, a shock that has nothing to do with Christ or the Crucifixion. The shock has to do with the Covenant, the intimacy of Jew and God. This intimacy is not sentimental; on the contrary, it is unfriendly. And it is the kind of intimacy that precludes religion itself—for Judaism is the minimum religion—and, secondarily, art itself. The unbelievable survival of the Jews must be seen against a background of Nothing, a people outside art or literature, a people in dread of the graven image, a people outside a Heaven and Hell, whose very sanctum sanctorum is an empty chamber. Yet this background of Nothing does not signify asceticism but the opposite, the sense of worldliness. The Jew is absolutely committed to the world. This people beyond philosophy, beyond art, virtually beyond religion, a stranger even to mysticism, finds itself at the very center of the divine manifestation—man. The Jew represents the primitive ego of the human race; he is its first exponent, the first, as it were, to accept the mission of the ego. This mission of the ego has proved all but suicidal, and yet the Jew cannot be erased from human consciousness, even by force.

I have referred to this consciousness as an obsession. In the nineteenth century, after the breakup of the ghetto system by Napoleon, the Jew was suddenly hurtled into the unknown modern freedom. His identity resultantly became confused: The German Jew grew more German than the Kaiser himself, the French Jew had to be reminded by the Dreyfus affair that he was still not French enough, and so on. The hideous blood purge of the Jews by Germany in the twentieth century revived throughout the world the spiritual image of the Jew, not as someone noble and good, or despicable and evil, not as the father of Western religions or the murderer of Christ, but as man essentially himself, beyond nationality, defenseless against the crushing impersonality of history. But the modern Jew, insofar as he is a Jew, remains intransigent and thankless, man in all his raw potentiality.

*x.*

The free modern Jew, celebrated so perfectly in the character of Leopold Bloom, is neither hero nor victim. He is man left over, after everything that can happen has happened.

As a third-generation American I grew up with the obsessive idea of personal liberty which engrosses all Americans except the oldest and richest families. As a Jew I grew up in an atmosphere of mysterious pride and sensitivity, an atmosphere in which even the greatest achievement was touched by a sense of the comic. Isolated within my own world, like a worm in an apple, I became a poet.

The poems here were written over a long period of time and are extracted mostly from volumes which have nothing to do with the present theme. But the undercurrent of most of my poems is the theme of the Jew, and for this reason I collect these examples now as a separate presentation.

*branding instead of beauty*

DEAD SEA SCROLLS

PART 1.

## The Alphabet

The letters of the Jews as strict as flames
Or little terrible flowers lean
Stubbornly upwards through the perfect ages,
Singing through solid stone the sacred names.
The letters of the Jews are black and clean
And lie in chain-line over Christian pages.
The chosen letters bristle like barbed wire
That hedge the flesh of man,
Twisting and tightening the book that warns.
These words, this burning bush, this flickering pyre
Unsacrifices the bled son of man
Yet plaits his crown of thorns.

Where go the tipsy idols of the Roman
Past synagogues of patient time,
Where go the sisters of the Gothic rose,
Where go the blue eyes of the Polish women
Past the almost natural crime,
Past the still speaking embers of ghettos,
There rise the tinder flowers of the Jews.
The letters of the Jews are dancing knives
That carve the heart of darkness seven ways.
These are the letters that all men refuse
And will refuse until the king arrives
And will refuse until the death of time
And all is rolled back in the book of days.

3.

## Israel

When I think of the liberation of Palestine,
When my eye conceives the great black English line
Spanning the world news of two thousand years,
My heart leaps forward like a hungry dog,
My heart is thrown back on its tangled chain,
My soul is hangdog in a Western chair.

When I think of the battle for Zion I hear
The drop of chains, the starting forth of feet,
And I remain chained in a Western chair.
My blood beats like a bird against a wall,
I feel the weight of prisons in my skull
Falling away; my forebears stare through stone.

When I see the name of Israel high in print
The fences crumble in my flesh; I sink
Deep in a Western chair and rest my soul.
I look the stranger clear to the blue depths
Of his unclouded eye. I say my name
Aloud for the first time unconsciously.

Speak of the tillage of a million heads
No more. Speak of the evil myth no more
Of one who harried Jesus on his way
Saying, *Go faster*. Speak no more
Of the yellow badge, *secta nefaria*.
Speak the name only of the living land.

4.

## The Dirty Word

The dirty word hops in the cage of the mind like the Pondicherry vulture, stomping with its heavy left claw on the sweet meat of the brain and tearing it with its vicious beak, ripping and chopping the flesh. Terrified, the small boy bears the big bird of the dirty word into the house, and grunting, puffing, carries it up the stairs to his own room in the skull. Bits of black feather cling to his clothes and his hair as he locks the staring creature in the dark closet.

All day the small boy returns to the closet to examine and feed the bird, to caress and kick the bird, that now snaps and flaps its wings savagely whenever the door is opened. How the boy trembles and delights at the sight of the white excrement of the bird! How the bird leaps and rushes against the walls of the skull, trying to escape from the zoo of the vocabulary! How wildly snaps the sweet meat of the brain in its rage.

And the bird outlives the man, being freed at the man's death-funeral by a word from the rabbi.

But I one morning went upstairs and opened the door and entered the closet and found in the cage of my mind the great bird dead. Softly I wept it and softly removed it and softly buried the body of the bird in the hollyhock garden of the house I lived in twenty years before. And out of the worn black feathers of the wing have I made pens to write these elegies, for I have outlived the bird, and I have murdered it in my early manhood.

5.

## The 151st Psalm

Are You looking for us? We are here.
Have You been gathering flowers, Elohim?
We are Your flowers, we have always been.
When will You leave us alone?
We are in America.
We have been here three hundred years.
And what new altar will You deck us with?


Whom are You following, Pillar of Fire?
What barn do You seek shelter in?
At whose gate do You whimper
In this great Palestine?
Whose wages do You take in this New World?
But Israel shall take what it shall take,
Making us ready for Your hungry Hand!


Immigrant God, You follow me;
You go with me, You are a distant tree;
You are the beast that lows in my heart's gates;
You are the dog that follows at my heel;
You are the table on which I lean;
You are the plate from which I eat.


Shepherd of the flocks of praise,
Youth of all youth, ancient of days,
Follow us.


6.

## The Olive Tree

Save for a lusterless honing-stone of moon
The sky stretches its flawless canopy
Blue as the blue silk of the Jewish flag
Over the valley and out to sea.
It is bluest just above the olive tree.
You cannot find in twisted Italy
So straight a one; it stands not on a crag,
Is not humpbacked with bearing in scored stone,
But perfectly erect in my front yard,
Oblivious of its fame. The fruit is hard,
Multitudinous, acid, tight on the stem;
The leaves ride boat-like in the brimming sun,
Going nowhere and scooping up the light.
It is the silver tree, the holy tree,
Tree of all attributes.

                    Now on the lawn
The olives fall by thousands, and I delight
To shed my tennis shoes and walk on them,
Pressing them coldly into the deep grass,
In love and reverence for the total loss.

7.

## The Synagogue

The synagogue dispirits the deep street,
Shadows the face of the pedestrian,
It is the adumbration of the Wall,
The stone survival that laments itself,
Our old entelechy of stubborn God,
Our calendar that marks a separate race.


The swift cathedral palpitates the blood,
The soul moves upward like a wing to meet
The pinnacles of saints. There flocks of thanks
In nooks of holy tracery arrive
And rested take their message in mid-air
Sphere after sphere into the papal heaven.


The altar of the Hebrews is a house,
No relic but a place, Sinai itself,
Not holy ground but factual holiness
Wherein the living god is resident.
Our scrolls are volumes of the thundered law
Sabbath by Sabbath wound by hand to read.


He knows Al-Eloah to whom the Arab
Barefooted falls on sands, on table roofs,
In latticed alleys underneath the egg
On wide mosaics, when the crier shrills.
O profitable curse, most sacred rug,
Your book is blindness and your sword is rust.


8.

And Judenhetze is the course of time;
We were rebellious, all but Abraham,
And skulked like Jonah, angry at the gourd.
Our days are captives in the minds of kings,
We stand in tens disjointed on the world,
Grieving the ribbon of a coast we hated.

Some choose the ethics of belief beyond
Even particular election. Some
In bland memorial churches modify
The architecture of the state, and heaven
Disfranchised watches, caput mortuum,
The human substance eating, voting, smiling.

The Jew has no bedecked magnificat
But sits in stricken ashes after death,
Refusing grace; his grave is flowerless,
He gutters in the tallow of his name.
At Rome the multiplying tapers sing
Life endless in the history of art.

And Zion womanless refuses grace
To the first woman as to Magdalene,
But half-remembers Judith or Rahab,
The shrewd good heart of Esther honors still,
And weeps for almost sacred Ruth, but doubts
Either full harlotry or the faultless birth.

Our wine is wine, our bread is harvest bread
That feeds the body and is not the body.
Our blessing is to wine but not the blood
Nor to sangreal the sacred dish. We bless
The whiteness of the dish and bless the water
And are not anthropophagous to him.

9.

The immanent son then came as one of us
And stood against the Ark. We have no prophets,
Our scholars are afraid. There have been friars,
Great healers, poets. The stars were terrible.
At the Sadducee court he touched our panic;
We were betrayed to sacrifice this man.


We live by virtue of philosophy,
Past love, and have our devious reward.
For faith he gave us land and took the land,
Thinking us exiles of all humankind.
Our name is yet the identity of God
That storms the falling altar of the world.

# The Phenomenon

How lovely it was, after the official fright,
To walk in the shadowy drifts, as if the clouds
Saturated with the obscurity of night
Had died and fallen piecemeal into shrouds.

What crepes there were, what sables heaped on stones,
What soft shakos on posts, tragically gay!
And oil-pool-flooded fields that blackly shone
The more black under the liquid eye of day!

It was almost warmer to the touch than sands
And sweeter-tasting than the white, and yet,
Walking, the children held their fathers' hands
Like visitors to a mine or parapet.

Then black it snowed again and while it fell
You could see the sun, an irritated rim
Wheeling through smoke; each from his shallow hell
Experienced injured vision growing dim.

But one day all was clear, and one day soon,
Sooner than those who witnessed it had died,
Nature herself forgot the phenomenon,
Her faulty snowfall brilliantly denied.

# *University*

To hurt the Negro and avoid the Jew
Is the curriculum. In mid-September
The entering boys, identified by hats,
Wander in a maze of mannered brick
   Where boxwood and magnolia brood
   And columns with imperious stance
   Like rows of ante-bellum girls
     Eye them, outlanders.


In whited cells, on lawns equipped for peace,
Under the arch, and lofty banister,
Equals shake hands, unequals blankly pass;
The exemplary weather whispers, "Quiet, quiet"
   And visitors on tiptoe leave
   For the raw North, the unfinished West,
   As the young, detecting an advantage,
     Practice a face.


Where, on their separate hill, the colleges,
Like manor houses of an older law,
Gaze down embankments on a land in fee,
The Deans, dry spinsters over family plate,
   Ring out the English name like coin,
   Humor the snob and lure the lout.
   Within the precincts of this world
     Poise is a club.

But on the neighboring range, misty and high,
The past is absolute: some luckless race
Dull with inbreeding and conformity
Wears out its heart, and comes barefoot and bad
   For charity or jail. The scholar
   Sanctions their obsolete disease;
   The gentleman revolts with shame
     At his ancestor.


And the true nobleman, once a democrat,
Sleeps on his private mountain. He was one
Whose thought was shapely and whose dream was broad;
This school he held his art and epitaph.
   But now it takes from him his name,
   Falls open like a dishonest look,
   And shows us, rotted and endowed,
     Its senile pleasure.

*13.*

## Washington Cathedral

From summer and the wheel-shaped city
 That sweats like a swamp and wrangles on
 Its melting streets, white mammoth Forums,
And political hotels with awnings, caryatids;
Past barricaded embassies with trees
 That shed trash and parch his eyes,
To here, the acres of superior quiet,
 Shadow and damp, the tourist comes,
 And, cooled by stones and darkness, stares.


 Tall as a lover's night, the nave
 Broods over him, irradiates,
And stars of color out of painted glass
Shoot downward on apostles and on chairs
Huddled by hundreds under altar rails.
Yet it is only Thursday; there are no prayers,


But exclamations. The lady invokes by name
 The thousand-odd small sculptures, spooks,
 New angels, pitted roods; she gives
The inventory of relics to his heart
That aches with history and astonishment:
He gives a large coin to a wooden coffer.

14.

Outside, noon blazes in his face like guns.
He goes down by the Bishop's walk, the dial,
   The expensive grass, the Byzantine bench,
While stark behind him a red naked crane
   Hangs over the unfinished transept,
A Cubist hen rivaling the Gothic School.


Whether he sees the joke; whether he cares;
Whether he tempts a vulgar miracle,
Some deus ex machina, this is his choice,
A shrine of whispers and tricky penumbras.
   Therefore he votes again for the paid
Clergy, the English hint, the bones of Wilson
Crushed under tons of fake magnificence.
   Nor from the zoo of his instincts
   Come better than crude eagles: now
He cannot doubt that violent obelisk
And Lincoln whittled to a fool's colossus.
This church and city triumph in his eyes.
He is only a good alien, nominally happy.


15.

# The Tingling Back

Sometimes deeply immured in white-washed tower
    quiet at ink and thinking book,
        alone with my own smoke,
the blood at rest, the body far below,
    swiftly there falls an angry shower
        of arrows upon my back,
like bees or electric needles run amok
    between my flesh and shirt. I know
        then I have touched the pain
of amour-propre, of something yesterday
    I said and I should not have said,
        I did and must not do.
These needles wing their insights from my brain
    and through and through my flesh they play
        to prick my skin with red
letters of shame and blue blurs of tattoo.
    I sweat and take my medicine
        for one must be sincere
and study one's sincerity like a crime:
    to be the very last to smile,
        the first one to begin
(when danger streaks the atmosphere) to fear,
    to pocket praises like a dime,
        to pet the crocodile,
to see a foreign agony as stone,
    to ravel dreams in crowded room,
        to let the hair grow tall,
to skin the eye and thrust it to the wind.
    Yet if I stood with God alone
        inside the blinding tomb

16.

I would not feel embarrassment at all
        nor those hot needles of the mind
                which are so clean. I'd ask
not if I'd known the tissue of my will
        and scarified my body white,
                but whether, insincere,
I'd grown to the simplicity of a mask;
        and if in natural error still
                whether my fingers might
destroy the true and keep the error **near.**

17.

# Travelogue for Exiles

Look and remember. Look upon this sky;
Look deep and deep into the sea-clean air,
The unconfined, the terminus of prayer.
Speak now and speak into the hallowed dome.
What do you hear? What does the sky reply?
*The heavens are taken: this is not your home.*


Look and remember. Look upon this sea;
Look down and down into the tireless tide.
What of a life below, a life inside,
A tomb, a cradle in the curly foam?
The waves arise; sea-wind and sea agree
*The waters are taken: this is not your home.*


Look and remember. Look upon this land,
Far, far across the factories and the grass.
Surely, there, surely, they will let you pass.
Speak then and ask the forest and the loam.
What do you hear? What does the land command?
*The earth is taken: this is not your home.*

## Lord, I Have Seen Too Much

Lord, I have seen too much for one who sat
In quiet at his window's luminous eye
And puzzled over house and street and sky,
Safe only in the narrowest habitat;
Who studied peace as if the world were flat,
The edge of nature linear and dry,
But faltered at each brilliant entity
Drawn like a prize from some magician's hat.

Too suddenly this lightning is disclosed:
Lord, in a day the vacuum of Hell,
The mouth of blood, the ocean's ragged jaw,
More than embittered Adam ever saw
When driven from Eden to the East to dwell,
The lust of godhead hideously exposed!

PART 2.

## Messias

Alone in the darkling apartment the boy
Was reading poetry when the doorbell rang;
The sound sped to his ear and winged his joy,
The book leaped from his lap on broken wing.


Down the gilt stairwell then he peered
Where an old man of patriarchal race
Climbed in an eastern language with his beard
A black halo around his paper face.


His glasses spun with vision and his hat
Was thick with fur in the August afternoon;
His silk suit crackled heavily with light
And in his hand a rattling canister shone.


Bigger he grew and softer the root words
Of the hieratic language of his heart,
And faced the boy, who flung the entrance wide
And fled in terror from the nameless hurt.


Past every door like a dead thing he swam,
Past the entablatures of the kitchen walls,
Down the red ringing of the fire escape
Singing with sun, to the green grass he came,


23.

Sickeningly green, leaving the man to lurch
Bewildered through the house and seat himself
In the sacrificial kitchen after his march,
To study the strange boxes on the shelf.


There mother found him mountainous and alone,
Mumbling some singsong in a monotone,
Crumbling breadcrumbs in his scholar's hand
That wanted a donation for the Holy Land.

# The Confirmation

When mothers weep and fathers richly proud
Worship on Sunday morning their tall son
And girls in white like angels in a play
    Tiptoe between the potted palms
    And all the crimson windows pray,
      The preacher bound in black
Opens his hands like pages of a book
    And holds the black and crimson law
      For every boy to look.


Last night between the chapters of a dream,
The photograph still sinning in the drawer,
The boy awoke; the moon shone in the yard
    On hairy hollyhocks erect
    And buds of roses pink and hard
      And on the solid wall
A square of light like movies fell to pose
    An actress naked in the night
      As hollyhock and rose.


And to confirm his sex, breathless and white
With benediction self-bestowed he knelt
Oh tightly married to his childish grip,
    And unction smooth as holy-oil
    Fell from the vessel's level lip
      Upon the altar-cloth;
Like Easter boys the blood sang in his head
    And all night long the tallow beads
      Like tears dried in the bed.

25.

Come from the church, you parents and you girls,
And walk with kisses and with happy jokes
Beside this man. Be doubly proud, you priest,
  Once for his passion in the rose,
  Once for his body self-released;
    And speak aloud of her
Who in the perfect consciousness of joy
  Stood naked in the electric light
    And woke the hidden boy.

## The Jew at Christmas Eve

I see the thin bell-ringer standing at corners
Fine as a breath, in cloth of red,
With eyes afar and long arm of a reed
Weakly waving a religious bell,
Under the boom of caroling hours
I see the thin bell-ringer standing still,
Breasting the prosperous tide on the Christmas pave.

I see the thin bell-ringer repeating himself
From corner to corner, year to year,
Struggling to stand beneath the windy blare
Of horns that carol out of walls.
He would attract a crying waif
Or garrulous old woman down-at-heels
Or a pair of lovers on the icy pave.

Whom do you summon, Santa of the spare?
Whom do you summon, arm of a reed?
Whom do you cheer with ringing and whom chide,
And who stops at the tripod at your side
And wishes you the time of year?
A few who feed the cauldron of the unfed,
The iron cauldron on the fireless pave.

I see the thin bell-ringer as a flame
Of scarlet, trying to throw the flame
With each sweep of the bell. The tide pours on
And wets the ringer in cloth of red
And parts around the ringer of flame
With eyes afar and long arm of a reed
Who shakes the fire on the snowy pave.

27.

## The First Time

Behind shut doors, in shadowy quarantine,
There shines the lamp of iodine and rose
That stains all love with its medicinal bloom.
This boy, who is no more than seventeen,
Not knowing what to do, takes off his clothes
As one might in a doctor's anteroom.

Then in a cross-draft of fear and shame
Feels love hysterically burn away,
A candle swimming down to nothingness
Put out by its own wetted gusts of flame,
And he stands smooth as uncarved ivory
Heavily curved for some expert caress.

And finally sees the always open door
That is invisible till the time has come,
And half falls through as through a rotten wall
To where chairs twist with dragons from the floor
And the great bed drugged with its own perfume
Spreads its carnivorous flower-mouth for all.

The girl is sitting with her back to him;
She wears a black thing and she rakes her hair,
Hauling her round face upward like moonrise;
She is younger than he, her angled arms are slim
And like a country girl her feet are bare.
She watches him behind her with old eyes,


Transfixing him in space like some grotesque,
Far, far from her where he is still alone
And being here is more and more untrue.
Then she turns round, as one turns at a desk,
And looks at him, too naked and too soon,
And almost gently asks: *Are you a Jew?*

29.

## Christmas Eve: Australia

The wind blows hot. English and foreign birds
And insects different as their fish excite
The would-be calm. The usual flocks and herds
Parade in permanent quiet out of sight,
And there one crystal like a grain of light
Sticks in the crucible of day and cools.
A cloud burnt to a crisp at some great height
Sips at the dark condensing in deep pools.


I smoke and read my Bible and chew gum,
Thinking of Christ and Christmas of last year,
And what those quizzical soldiers standing near
Ask of the war and Christmases to come,
And sick of causes and the tremendous blame
Curse lightly and pronounce your serious name.

# Sunday: New Guinea

The bugle sounds the measured call to prayers,
The band starts bravely with a clarion hymn,
From every side, singly, in groups, in pairs,
Each to his kind of service comes to worship Him.


Our faces washed, our hearts in the right place,
We kneel or stand or listen from our tents;
Half-naked natives with their kind of grace
Move down the road with balanced staffs like mendicants.


And over the hill the guns bang like a door
And planes repeat their mission in the heights.
The jungle outmaneuvers creeping war
And crawls within the circle of our sacred rites.


I long for our disheveled Sundays home,
Breakfast, the comics, news of latest crimes,
Talk without reference, and palindromes,
Sleep and the Philharmonic and the ponderous *Times*.


I long for lounging in the afternoons
Of clean intelligent warmth, my brother's mind,
Books and thin plates and flowers and shining spoons,
And your love's presence, snowy, beautiful, and kind.


*31.*

# The Leg

Among the iodoform, in twilight-sleep,
*What have I lost?* he first inquires,
Peers in the middle distance where a pain,
Ghost of a nurse, hazily moves, and day,
Her blinding presence pressing in his eyes
And now his ears. They are handling him
With rubber hands. He wants to get up.

One day beside some flowers near his nose
He will be thinking, *When will I look at it?*
And pain, still in the middle distance, will reply,
*At what?* and he will know it's gone,
O where! and begin to tremble and cry.
He will begin to cry as a child cries
Whose puppy is mangled under a screaming wheel.

Later, as if deliberately, his fingers
Begin to explore the stump. He learns a shape
That is comfortable and tucked in like a sock.
This has a sense of humor, this can despise
The finest surgical limb, the dignity of limping,
The nonsense of wheel chairs. Now he smiles to the wall:
The amputation becomes an acquisition.

For the leg is wondering where he is (all is not lost)
And surely he has a duty to the leg;
He is its injury, the leg is his orphan,
He must cultivate the mind of the leg,
Pray for the part that is missing, pray for peace
In the image of man, pray, pray for its safety,
And after a little it will die quietly.

The body, what is it, Father, but a sign
To love the force that grows us, to give back
What in Thy palm is senselessness and mud?
Knead, knead the substance of our understanding
Which must be beautiful in flesh to walk,
That if Thou take me angrily in hand
And hurl me to the shark, I shall not die!

33.

*Five Self-Portraits*

I    I was born downtown on a wintry day
      And under the roof where Poe expired;
    Tended by nuns my mother lay
      Dark-haired and beautiful and tired.


    Doctors and cousins paid their call,
      The rabbi and my father helped.
    A crucifix burned on the wall
      Of the bright room where I was whelped.


    At one week all my family prayed,
      Stuffed wine and cotton in my craw;
    The rabbi blessed me with a blade
      According to the Mosaic Law.


    The white steps blazed in Baltimore
      And cannas and white statuary.
    I went home voluble and sore
      Influenced by Abraham and Mary.

II At one the Apocalypse had spoken,
Von Moltke fell, I was housebroken.

At two how could I understand
The murder of Archduke Ferdinand?

France was involved with history,
I with my thumbs when I was three.

A sister came, we neared a war,
Paris was shelled when I was four.

I joined in our peach-kernel drive
For poison gas when I was five.

At six I cheered the big parade,
Burned sparklers and drank lemonade.

At seven I passed at school though I
Was far too young to say *Versailles*.

At eight the boom began to tire,
I tried to set our house on fire.

The Bolsheviks had drawn the line,
Lenin was stricken, I was nine.

—What evils do not retrograde
To my first odious decade?

III    Saints by whose pages I would swear,
       My Zarathustra, Edward Lear,
   Ulysses, Werther, fierce Flaubert,
      Where are my books of yesteryear?


   Sixteen and sixty are a pair;
      We twice live by philosophies;
   My marginalia of the hair,
      Are you at one with Socrates?


   Thirty subsides yet does not dare,
      Sixteen and sixty bang their fists.
   How is it that I no longer care
      For Kant and the Transcendentalists?


   Public libraries lead to prayer,
      EN APXH ἦν ὁ λόγος—still
   Eliot and John are always there
      To tempt our admirari nil.

IV     I lived in a house of panels,
       Victorian, darkly made;
    A virgin in bronze and marble
       Leered from the balustrade.


    The street was a tomb of virtues,
       Autumnal for dreams and haunts;
    I gazed from the polished windows
       Toward a neighborhood of aunts.


    Mornings I practiced piano,
       Wrote elegies and sighed;
    The evenings were conversations
       Of poetry and suicide.


    Weltschmerz and mysticism,
       What tortures we undergo!
    I loved with the love of Heinrich
       And the poison of Edgar Poe.

V    I plucked the bougainvillaea
       In Queensland in time of war;
    The train stopped at the station
       And I reached it from my door.


    I have never kept a flower
       And this one I never shall
    I thought as I laid the blossom
       In the leaves of *Les Fleurs du Mal*.


    I read my book in the desert
       In the time of death and fear,
    The flower slipped from the pages
       And fell to my lap, my dear.


    I sent it inside my letter,
       The purplest kiss I knew,
    And thus you abused my passion
       With "A most Victorian Jew."

38.

## V-Letter

I love you first because your face is fair,
    Because your eyes Jewish and blue,
Set sweetly with the touch of foreignness
Above the cheekbones, stare rather than dream.
Often your countenance recalls a boy
    Blue-eyed and small, whose silent mischief
Tortured his parents and compelled my hate
      To wish his ugly death.
Because of this reminder, my soul's trouble,
And for your face, so often beautiful,
    I love you, wish you life.

I love you first because you wait, because
    For your own sake, I cannot write
Beyond these words. I love you for these words
That sting and creep like insects and leave filth.
I love you for the poverty you cry
    And I bend down with tears of steel
That melt your hand like wax, not for this war
    The droplets shattering
Those candle-glowing fingers of my joy,
But for your name of agony, my love,
    That cakes my mouth with salt.

And all your imperfections and perfections
    And all your magnitude of grace
And all this love explained and unexplained
Is just a breath. I see you woman-size
And this looms larger and more goddess-like
    Than silver goddesses on screens.
I see you in the ugliness of light,

39.

Yet you are beautiful,
And in the dark of absence your full length
Is such as meets my body to the full
        Though I am starved and huge.


You turn me from these days as from a scene
        Out of an open window far
Where lies the foreign city and the war.
You are my home and in your spacious love
I dream to march as under flaring flags
        Until the door is gently shut.
Give me the tearless lesson of your pride,
        Teach me to live and die
As one deserving anonymity,
The mere devotion of a house to keep
        A woman and a man.


Give me the free and poor inheritance
        Of our own kind, not furniture
Of education, nor the prophet's pose,
The general cause of words, the hero's stance,
The ambitions incommensurable with flesh,
        But the drab makings of a room
Where sometimes in the afternoon of thought
        The brief and blinding flash
May light the enormous chambers of your will
And show the gracious Parthenon that time
        Is ever measured by.


As groceries in a pantry gleam and smile
        Because they are important weights
Bought with the metal minutes of your pay,
So do these hours stand in solid rows,

40.

The dowry for a use in common life.
    I love you first because your years
Lead to my matter-of-fact and simple death
        Or to our open marriage,
And I pray nothing for my safety back,
Not even luck, because our love is whole
        Whether I live or fail.

# The Ham-Bone of a Saint

I     Much of transfiguration that we hear,
      The ballet of the atoms, the second law
      Of thermodynamics, Isis, and the queer

      Fertilization of fish, the Catholic's awe
      For the life-cycle of the Nazarene,
      His wife whom sleeping Milton thought he saw;

      Much of the resurrection that we've seen
      And taken part in, like the Passion Play,
      All of autumnal red and April green,

      To those who walk in work from day to day,
      To economic and responsible man,
      All, all is substance. Life that lets him stay

      Uses his substance kindly while she can
      But drops him lifeless after his one span.

II  What lives? the proper creatures in their homes?
    A weed? the white and giddy butterfly?
    Bacteria? necklaces of chromosomes?


    What lives? the breathing bell of the clear sky?
    The crazed bull of the sea? Andean crags?
    Armies that plunge into themselves to die?


    People? A sacred relic wrapped in rags,
    The ham-bone of a saint, the winter rose,
    Do these?—And is there not a hand that drags


    The bottom of the universe for those
    Who still perhaps are breathing? Listen well,
    There lives a quiet like a cathedral close


    At the soul's center where substance cannot dwell
    And life flowers like music from a bell.

III    Writing, I crushed an insect with my nail
And thought nothing at all. A bit of wing
Caught my eye then, a gossamer so frail

And exquisite, I saw in it a thing
That scorned the grossness of the thing I wrote.
It hung upon my finger like a sting.

A leg I noticed next, fine as a mote,
"And on this frail eyelash he walked," I said,
"And climbed and walked like any mountain goat."

And in this mood I sought the little head,
But it was lost; then in my heart a fear
Cried out, "A life—why beautiful, why dead!"

It was a mite that held itself most dear,
So small I could have drowned it with a tear.

## Teasing the Nuns

Up in the elevator went the nuns
    Wild as a cage of undomestic ducks,
Turning and twittering their unclipped hats,
    Gay in captivity, a flirtatious flock
Of waterfowl tipped with black
    Above the traffic and its searing suns.
Higher and higher in the wall we flew
    Hauled on by rosaries and split strands of hair,
Myself in the center sailing like Sinbad
    Yanked into heaven by a hairy Roc;
Whence we emerged into a towery cell
    Where holy cross was splayed upon the wall
In taxidermy of the eternal. They
    Bedecked in elegant bird-names dropped
Curtsies, I thought, and merrily sat
    And fixed their gaze on mine that floated out
Between them and their poised hawk.

"Sisters," I said.—And then I stopped.

# The Crucifix in the Filing Cabinet

Out of the filing cabinet of true steel
That saves from fire my rags of letters, bills,
Manuscripts, contracts, all the trash of praise
Which one acquires to prove and prove his days;

Out of the drawer that rolls on hidden wheels
I drew a crucifix with beaded chain,
Still new and frightened-looking and absurd.
I picked it up as one picks up a bird

And placed it on my palm. It formed a pile
Like a small mound of stones on which there stands
A tree crazy with age, and on the tree
Some ancient teacher hanging by his hands.

I found a velvet bag sewn by the Jews
For holy shawls and frontlets and soft thongs
That bind the arm at morning for great wrongs
Done in a Pharaoh's time. The crucifix

I dropped down in the darkness of this pouch,
Thought tangled with thought and chain with chain,
Till time untie the dark with greedy look,
Crumble the cross and bleed the leathery vein.

46.

## My Grandmother

My grandmother moves to my mind in context of sorrow
And, as if apprehensive of near death, in black;
Whether erect in chair, her dry and corded throat
    harangued by grief,
Or at ragged book bent in Hebrew prayer,
Or gentle, submissive, and in tears to strangers;
Whether in sunny parlor or back of drawn blinds.


Though time and tongue made any love disparate,
On daguerreotype with classic perspective
Beauty I sigh and soften at is hers.
I pity her life of deaths, the agony of her own,
But most that history moved her through
Stranger lands and many houses,
Taking her exile for granted, confusing
The tongues and tasks of her children's children.

# Jew

The name is immortal but only the name, for the rest
Is a nose that can change in the weathers of time or persist
Or die out in confusion or model itself on the best.


But the name is a language itself that is whispered and hissed
Through the houses of ages, and ever a language the same,
And ever and ever a blow on our heart like a fist.


And this last of our dream in the desert, O curse of our name,
Is immortal as Abraham's voice in our fragment of prayer
Adonai, Adonai, for our bondage of murder and shame!


And the word for the murder of God will cry out on the air
Though the race is no more and the temples are closed of our
        will
And the peace is made fast on the earth and the earth is made
        fair;


Our name is impaled in the heart of the world on a hill
Where we suffer to die by the hands of ourselves, and to kill.


50.

# The Southerner

He entered with the authority of politeness
And the jokes died in the air. A well-made blaze
Grew round the main log in the fireplace
Spontaneously. I watched its brightness
Spread to the altered faces of my guests.
They did not like the Southerner. I did.
A liberal felt that someone should forbid
That soft voice making its soft arrests.


As when a Negro or a prince extends
His hand to an average man, and the mind
Speeds up a minute and then drops behind,
So did the conversation of my friends.
I was amused by this respectful awe
Which those hotly deny who have no prince.
I watched the frown, the stare, and the wince
Recede into attention, the arms thaw.


I saw my southern evil memories
Raped from my mind before my eyes, my youth
Practicing caste, perfecting the untruth
Of staking honor on the wish to please.
I saw my honor's paradox:
Grandpa, the saintly Jew, keeping his beard
In difficult Virginia, yet endeared
Of blacks and farmers, although orthodox.

51.

The nonsense of the gracious lawn,
The fall of hollow columns in the pines,
Do these deceive more than the rusted signs
Of Jesus on the road? Can they go on
In the timeless manner of all gentlefolk
There in a culture rotted and unweeded
Where the black yoni of the South is seeded
By crooked men in denims thin as silk?


They do go on, denying still the fall
Of Richmond and man, who gently live
On the street above the violence, fugitive,
Graceful, and darling, who recall
The heartbroken country once about to flower,
Full of black poison, beautiful to smell,
Who know how to conform, how to compel,
And how from the best bush to receive a flower.

## The Murder of Moses

By reason of despair we set forth behind you
And followed the pillar of fire like a doubt,
To hold to belief wanted a sign,
Called the miracle of the staff and the plagues
Natural phenomena.

We questioned the expediency of the march,
Gossiped about you. What was escape
To the fear of going forward and Pharaoh's wheels?
When the chariots mired and the army flooded
Our cry of horror was one with theirs.

You always went alone, a little ahead,
Prophecy disturbed you, you were not a fanatic.
The women said you were meek, the men
Regarded you as a typical leader.
You and your black wife might have been foreigners.

We even discussed your parentage; were you really a Jew?
We remembered how Joseph had made himself a prince,
All of us shared in the recognition
Of his skill of management, sense of propriety,
Devotion to his brothers and Israel.

We hated you daily. Our children died. The water spilled.
It was as if you were trying to lose us one by one.
Our wandering seemed the wandering of your mind,
The cloud believed we were tireless,
We expressed our contempt and our boredom openly.

53.

At last you ascended the rock; at last returned.
Your anger that day was probably His.
When we saw you come down from the mountain, your skin alight
And the stones of our law flashing,
We fled like animals and the dancers scattered.


We watched where you overturned the calf on the fire,
We hid when you broke the tablets on the rock,
We wept when we drank the mixture of gold and water.
We had hoped you were lost or had left us.
This was the day of our greatest defilement.


You were simple of heart; you were sorry for Miriam,
You reasoned with Aaron, who was your enemy.
However often you cheered us with songs and prayers
We cursed you again. The serpents bit us,
And mouth to mouth you entreated the Lord for our sake.


At the end of it all we gave you the gift of death.
Invasion and generalship were spared you.
The hand of our direction, resignedly you fell,
And while officers prepared for the river-crossing
The One God blessed you and covered you with earth.


Though you were mortal and once committed murder
You assumed the burden of the covenant,
Spoke for the world and for our understanding.
Converse with God made you a thinker,
Taught us all early justice, made us a race.


54.

# Shylock

*Ho, no, no, no, no, my meaning in saying he is a good man is to
have you understand me, that he is sufficient.*—THE MERCHANT OF
VENICE

Home from the court he locked the door and sat
In the evil darkness, suddenly composed.
The knife shone dimly on the table and his eyes
Like candles in an empty room
Shone hard at nothing. Yet he appeared to smile.

Then he took up his talith and his hat
And prayed mechanically and absently closed
His fingers on the knife. If he could realize
His actual defeat or personal doom
He must die or change or show that he was vile.

Nevertheless he would remain and live,
Submit to baptism, pay his fines,
Appear in the Rialto as early as tomorrow,
Not innocently but well aware
That his revenge is an accomplished fact.

And poverty itself would help to give
Humility to his old designs.
His fallen reputation would help borrow
A credit of new hate; for nothing will repair
This open breach of nature, cruel and wracked.

55.

His daughter lies with swine, and the old rat
Tubal will be obsequious
To buy off his disgrace and bargain on his shame.
Despair can teach him nothing at all:
Gold he hates more than he hates Jesus' crown.


The logic of Balthasar will fall flat
On heaven's hearing. Incurious
As to the future, totally clear of blame,
He takes his ledgers out of the wall
And lights them with a taper and sits down.

56.

## The Progress of Faust

He was born in Deutschland, as you would suspect,
And graduated in magic from Cracow
In Fifteen Five. His portraits show a brow
Heightened by science. The eye is indirect,
As of bent light upon a crooked soul,
And that he bargained with the Prince of Shame
For pleasures intellectually foul
Is known by every court that lists his name.

His frequent disappearances are put down
To visits in the regions of the damned
And to the periodic deaths he shammed,
But, unregenerate and in Doctor's gown,
He would turn up to lecture at the fair
And do a minor miracle for a fee.
Many a life he whispered up the stair
To teach the black art of anatomy.

He was as deaf to angels as an oak
When, in the fall of Fifteen Ninety-four,
He went to London and crashed through the floor
In mock damnation of the playgoing folk.
Weekending with the scientific crowd,
He met Sir Francis Bacon and helped draft
"Colours of Good and Evil" and read aloud
An obscene sermon at which no one laughed.

He toured the Continent for a hundred years
And subsidized among the peasantry
The puppet play, his tragic history;

With a white glove he boxed the Devil's ears
And with a black his own. Tired of this,
He published penny poems about his sins,
In which he placed the heavy emphasis
On the white glove which, for a penny, wins.

Some time before the hemorrhage of the Kings
Of France, he turned respectable and taught;
Quite suddenly everything that he had thought
Seemed to grow scholars' beards and angels' wings.
It was the Overthrow. On Reason's throne
He sat with the fair Phrygian on his knees
And called all universities his own,
As plausible a figure as you please.

Then back to Germany as the sages' sage
To preach comparative science to the young
Who came from every land in a great throng
And knew they heard the master of the age.
When for a secret formula he paid
The Devil another fragment of his soul,
His scholars wept, and several even prayed
That Satan would restore him to them whole.

Backwardly tolerant, Faustus was expelled
From the Third Reich in Nineteen Thirty-nine.
His exit caused the breaching of the Rhine,
Except for which the frontier might have held.
Five years unknown to enemy and friend
He hid, appearing on the sixth to pose
In an American desert at war's end
Where, at his back, a dome of atoms rose.

# Mongolian Idiot

A dog that spoke, a monster born of sheep
We mercilessly kill, and kill the thought,
Yet house the parrot and let the centaur go,
These being to their nature and those not.
We laugh at apes, that never quite succeed
      At eating soup or wearing hats.


Adam had named so many but not this,
This that would name a curse when it had come,
Unfinished man, or witch, or myth, or sin,
Not ever father and never quite a son.
Ape had outstripped him, dog and darling lamb
      And all the kindergarten beasts.


Enter the bare room of his mind and count
His store of words with letters large and black;
See how he handles clumsily those blocks
With swans and sums; his colored picture books.
At thirty-five he squeals to see the ball
      Bounce in the air and roll away.


Pity and fear we give this innocent
Who maimed his mother's beautiful instinct;
But she would say, "My body had a dog;
I bore the ape and nursed the crying sheep.
He is my kindness and my splendid gift
      Come from all life and for all life."

59.

# The Convert

Deep in the shadowy bethel of the tired mind,
Where spooks and death lights ride, and Marys, too,
Materialize like senseless ectoplasm
Smiling in blue, out of the blue,
Quite gradually, on a common afternoon,
With no more inner fanfare than a sigh,
With no cross in the air, drizzle of blood,
Beauty of blinding voices from up high,
The man surrenders reason to the ghost
And enters church, via the vestry room.

The groan of positive science, hiss of friends,
Substantiate what doctors call
His rather shameful and benign disease,
But ecumenical heaven clearly sees
His love, his possibilities.
O victory of the Unintelligence,
What mystic rose developing from rock
Is more a miracle than this overthrow?
What Constitution ever promised more
Than his declared insanity?

Yet he shall be less perfect than before,
Being no longer neutral to the Book
But answerable. What formerly were poems,
Precepts, and commonplaces now are laws,
Dantean atlases, and official news.
The dust of ages settles on his mind
And in his ears he hears the click of beads
Adding, adding, adding like a prayer machine
His heartfelt sums. Upon his new-found knees
He treasures up the gold of never-ending day.

And there he followed shyly to observe.
She was already turning beautiful.


## III. THE KISS

The first kiss was with stumbling fingertips.
Their bodies grazed each other as if by chance
And touched and untouched in a kind of dance.
Second, they found out touching with their lips.

Some obscure angel, pausing on his course,
Shed such a brightness on the face of Eve
That Adam in grief was ready to believe
He had lost her love. The third kiss was by force.

Their lips formed foreign, unimagined oaths
When speaking of the Tree of Guilt. So wide
Their mouths, they drank each other from inside.
A gland of honey burst within their throats.

But something rustling hideously overhead,
They jumped up from the fourth caress and hid.


## IV. THE TREE OF GUILT

Why, on her way to the oracle of Love,
Did she not even glance up at the Tree
Of Life, that giant with the whitish cast
And glinting leaves and berries of dull gray,

65.

As though covered with mold? But who would taste
The medicine of immortality,
And who would "be as God"? And in what way?


So she came breathless to the lowlier one
And like a priestess of the cult she knelt,
Holding her breasts in token for a sign,
And prayed the spirit of the burdened bough
That the great power of the tree be seen
And lift itself out of the Tree of Guilt
Where it had hidden in the leaves till now.


Or did she know already? Had the peacock
Rattling its quills, glancing its thousand eyes
At her, the iridescence of the dove,
Stench of the he-goat, everything that joins
Told her the mystery? It was not enough,
So from the tree the snake began to rise
And dropt its head and pointed at her loins.


She fell and hid her face and still she saw
The spirit of the tree emerge and slip
Into the open sky until it stood
Straight as a standing-stone, and spilled its seed.
And all the seed were serpents of the good.
Again he seized the snake and from its lip
It spat the venomous evil of the deed.


And it was over. But the woman lay
Stricken with what she knew, ripe in her thought
Like a fresh apple fallen from the limb
And rotten, like a fruit that lies too long.
This way she rose, ripe-rotten in her prime

66.

And spurned the cold thing coiled against her foot
And called her husband, in a kind of song.

## V. THE CONFESSION

As on the first day her first word was *thou.*
He waited while she said, "Thou art the tree."
And while she said, almost accusingly,
Looking at nothing, "Thou art the fruit I took."
She seemed smaller by inches as she spoke,
And Adam wondering touched her hair and shook,
Half understanding. He answered softly, "How?"

And for the third time, in the third way, Eve:
"The tree that rises from the middle part
Of the garden." And almost tenderly, "Thou art
The garden. *We.*" Then she was overcome,
And Adam coldly, lest he should succumb
To pity, standing at the edge of doom,
Comforted her like one about to leave.

She sensed departure and she stood aside
Smiling and bitter. But he asked again,
"How did you eat? With what thing did you sin?"
And Eve with body slackened and uncouth,
"Under the tree I took the fruit of truth
From an angel. I ate it with my other mouth."
And saying so, she did not know she lied.

It was the man who suddenly released
From doubt, wept in the woman's heavy arms,
Those double serpents, subtly winding forms
That climb and drop about the manly boughs;
And dry with weeping, fiery and aroused,
Fell on her face to slake his terrible thirst
And bore her body earthward like a beast.

67.

## VI. SHAME

The hard blood falls back in the manly fount,
The soft door closes under Venus' mount,
The ovoid moon moves to the Garden's side
And dawn comes, but the lovers have not died.
They have not died but they have fallen apart
In sleep, like equal halves of the same heart.

How to teach shame? How to teach nakedness
To the already naked? How to express
Nudity? How to open innocent eyes
And separate the innocent from the wise?
And how to re-establish the guilty tree
In infinite gardens of humanity?

By marring the image, by the black device
Of the goat-god, by the clown of Paradise,
By fruits of cloth and by the navel's bud,
By itching tendrils and by strings of blood,
By ugliness, by the shadow of our fear,
By ridicule, by the fig-leaf patch of hair.

Whiter than tombs, whiter than whitest clay,
Exposed beneath the whitening eye of day,
They awoke and saw the covering that reveals.
They thought they were changing into animals.
Like animals they bellowed terrible cries
And clutched each other, hiding each other's eyes.

## VII. EXILE

The one who gave the warning with his wings,
Still doubting them, held out the sword of flame

68.

Against the Tree of Whiteness as they came
Angrily, slowly by, like exiled kings,

And watched them at the broken-open gate
Stare in the distance long and overlong,
And then, like peasants, pitiful and strong,
Take the first step toward earth and hesitate.

For Adam raised his head and called aloud,
"My Father, who has made the garden pall,
Giving me all things and then taking all,
Who with your opposite nature has endowed

Woman, give us your hand for our descent.
Needing us greatly, even in our disgrace,
Guide us, for gladly do we leave this place
For our own land and wished-for banishment."

But woman prayed, "Guide us to Paradise."
Around them slunk the uneasy animals,
Strangely excited, uttering coughs and growls,
And bounded down into the wild abyss.

And overhead the last migrating birds,
Then empty sky. And when the two had gone
A slow half-dozen steps across the stone,
The angel came and stood among the shards

And called them, as though joyously, by name.
They turned in dark amazement and beheld
Eden ablaze with fires of red and gold,
The garden dressed for dying in cold flame,

And it was autumn, and the present world.

69.

# Notes

A few of the poems may require a word of explanation, either because of some obscurity in the text or because of a seeming irrelevancy to the collection as a whole. I hope, of course, that no one will need the notes.

*Israel, p. 4*

This poem was commissioned to be read at a celebration of the founding of the State of Israel in 1948. It was performed at a mass meeting in Baltimore in that year.

*The 151st Psalm, p. 6*

Commissioned to be performed for the celebration of the three-hundredth anniversary of the landing of the Jews in America.

*The Synagogue, p. 8*

The word "philosophy" here has the meaning of "stoical" in the vulgar sense. The image is that of the shrug.

*The Phenomenon, p. 11*

The poem refers to the world of the Nazis. Black has long been the official, as well as the symbolic color for Germany. The first black snowfall indicates the triumph of Hitler; the second the destruction of Germany. The closing quatrain is intended as a warning against the forgetfulness of history.

*The Leg, p. 32*

Freud speaks (it may be all too often) of "violent defloration" and "the fear of being eaten by the Father." In Freud's view, as in that of every Jew, mutilation, circumcision, and "the fear of being eaten" are all one. *The Leg* is a poem written during war and its subject is the wholeness even of the mutilated. The poem *Mongolian Idiot* has the same theme.

### V-Letter, p. 39

The title refers to a photostat miniature letter used by the U. S. Army.

### Teasing the Nuns, p. 45

The setting of the poem is a skyscraper of Loyola University in Chicago, where I taught a class in writing for several years. The theme of the poem is the essential inability of the Jew to speak to the nuns.

### The Murder of Moses, p. 53

Based on Freud's *Moses and Monotheism*. It is in this work that Freud says, "The unmentionable crime was replaced by the tenet of the somewhat shadowy conception of original sin." My poem originally was called *Moses*, and the reference to the "murder" was muted. See also the sonnet *Jew*.

### Shylock, p. 55

Attempts to brighten the character of Shylock by certain scholars and apologists seem to me absurd. Shylock represents not greed but hatred. As such he is a legitimate Shakespearean Jew, a mystery even to Shakespeare.

### Mongolian Idiot, p. 59

Among Jews he is accepted as a member of the household and is not shunned. In my childhood I was acquainted with a dozen of these unfortunates. One does not see them any more.

### Adam and Eve, p. 62

These poems were originally printed under the title *Eden Retold*. The poems in this series are not symbolic but literal interpretations. That is, I wrote them according to my own interpretation of the lines in Genesis, where they are first presented. Rilke says that Adam was *determined* to leave the Garden. My argument in the poem is that God determined him to leave it. Much of the imagery of the poems is drawn from the *Zohar* or central work of the cabala, some from the renegade Freudian, Wilhelm Reich. The viewpoint of the sequence, that man is for the world, not for the afterworld, is Jewish.

**A B O U T   T H E   A U T H O R**

KARL SHAPIRO was born in Baltimore, Maryland, on November 10, 1913, and attended the University of Virginia and Johns Hopkins University. When his first book, *Person, Place and Thing*, was published in 1942, Mr. Shapiro was already with the army in the South Pacific, where he remained until the spring of 1945. In 1946 he was appointed Consultant in Poetry at the Library of Congress, and then, in 1947, he joined the faculty of Johns Hopkins University, where he taught writing courses until he resigned in 1950 to become editor of *Poetry: A Magazine of Verse*. Mr. Shapiro is now Professor of English at the University of Nebraska, and is editor of *The Schooner*.

Mr. Shapiro's poems, essays and reviews have appeared in leading literary magazines all over the world. His second volume of verse, *V-Letter and Other Poems*, was awarded the Pulitzer Prize in 1945.